A GIFT OF

HELEN WEBER

DECEMBER 1996

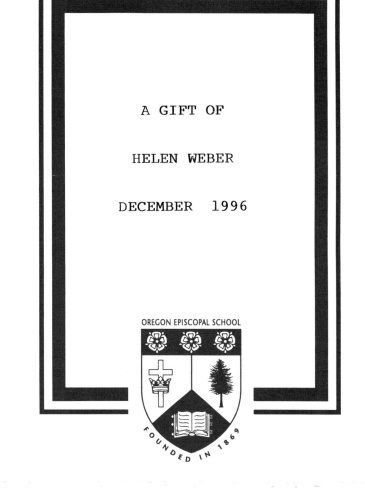

OREGON EPISCOPAL SCHOOL

FOUNDED IN 1869

VOICES · IN POETRY

SYLVIA PLATH

TEXT BY
LYNNE F. CHAPMAN

PHOTOGRAPHS BY

BENNO FRIEDMAN

CREATIVE EDUCATION

$\mathcal{D}$ying

Is an art, like everything else.

I do it exceptionally well.

I do it so it feels like hell.

I do it so it feels real.

I guess you could say I've a call.

From "Lady Lazarus"
Ariel

When Sylvia Plath wrote "Lady Lazarus" in 1962, she was only three months away from ending her life. She had already made one well-publicized suicide attempt at the age of twenty. Why was this extraordinarily gifted and successful woman obsessed with dying?

Plath lived an intense life, marked occasionally by great joy but more often by profound misery. With her characteristically strong feelings she despised herself for her shortcomings, grieved for her father's premature death, hated her husband for his betrayal of her, and resented her mother, on whom she depended for approval. In the end, she was too exhausted by these emotions to go on living.

Sylvia Plath's poetry—painfully personal, raw, often bitterly angry—is just as intense as she was and also arouses intense emotions in its readers. Feminists applaud its portrait of a victimized but not broken-spirited woman; romantics are moved by its tragedy; others are simply haunted by its imagery. Some readers are uncomfortable with, or even offended by, its subject matter. Yet few would dispute that Plath has earned a place among the most important American poets of the last half century.

Sylvia Plath at the age of twenty-one.

ARIEL

Stasis in darkness.

Then the substanceless blue

Pour of tor and distances.

God's lioness,

How one we grow,

Pivot of heels and knees!—The furrow

Splits and passes, sister to

The brown arc

Of the neck I cannot catch,

Nigger-eye

Berries cast dark

Hooks——

Black sweet blood mouthfuls,

Shadows.

Something else

Hauls me through air——

Thighs, hair;

Flakes from my heels.

White

Godiva, I unpeel——

Dead hands, dead stringencies.

And now I

Foam to wheat, a glitter of seas.

The child's cry

Melts in the wall.

And I

Am the arrow,

The dew that flies

Suicidal, at one with the drive

Into the red

Eye, the cauldron of morning.

From the collection *Ariel*

C H I L D H O O D

Sylvia Plath's father Otto and her mother Aurelia both came from poor immigrant families. Each of them had overcome deprivation and personal hardship, Otto to become a well-respected professor of entomology at Boston University and Aurelia a high school teacher of English and German.

Sylvia, born in Boston, Massachusetts, on October 27, 1932, gave her parents much cause for pride. She was an attractive, energetic child who was obviously intellectually gifted. Sensing early that the best way to get her parents' approval was to be an achiever, Sylvia began to read before she was three and to build models of structures such as the Taj Mahal out of blocks. When her brother Warren was born in 1935, the competitive Sylvia intensified her efforts to get noticed.

Although Sylvia wanted to please both her parents, she was most anxious to impress her father, who was a distant, remote man. Obsessed with his work, he rarely

ate meals with the children or played with them.

Otto became even more remote after he fell ill in 1936. Over the next four years his condition worsened. Increasingly tired and moody, he only saw his children for a few minutes each evening in his study. He avoided consulting a doctor about his condition, but when he stubbed his toe and gangrene quickly set in, a physician was finally called. The diagnosis was diabetes. But it was too late to save him, and he died in November 1940.

When eight-year-old Sylvia heard the news of her father's death, her first reaction was to cry in a fury, "I'll never speak to God again!" After this single outburst, however, she insisted on acting normally. Sylvia did not really mourn her father until almost twenty years later, while she was seeing a therapist for depression. Over the years her grief had changed into rage over what she saw as her father's "desertion." She vented this rage in perhaps her most famous poem, the astonishing "Daddy," written in 1962, in which she compares Otto Plath to a Nazi, a devil, and a vampire.

DADDY

You do not do, you do not do

Any more, black shoe

In which I have lived like a foot

For thirty years, poor and white,

Barely daring to breathe or Achoo.

Daddy, I have had to kill you.

You died before I had time——

Marble-heavy, a bag full of God,

Ghastly statue with one grey toe

Big as a Frisco seal

And a head in the freakish Atlantic

Where it pours bean green over blue

In the waters off beautiful Nauset.

I used to pray to recover you.

Ach, du.

In the German tongue, in the Polish town

Scraped flat by the roller

Of wars, wars, wars.

But the name of the town is common.

My Polack friend

Says there are a dozen or two.

So I never could tell where you

Put your foot, your root,

I never could talk to you.

The tongue stuck in my jaw.

It stuck in a barb wire snare.

Ich, ich, ich, ich,

I could hardly speak.

I thought every German was you.

And the language obscene

An engine, an engine

Chuffing me off like a Jew.

A Jew to Dachau, Auschwitz, Belsen.

I began to talk like a Jew.

I think I may well be a Jew.

The snows of the Tyrol, the clear beer of Vienna

Are not very pure or true.

With my gypsy ancestress and my weird luck

And my Taroc pack and my Taroc pack

I may be a bit of a Jew.

(continued)

I have always been scared of *you*,

With your Luftwaffe, your gobbledygoo.

And your neat moustache

And your Aryan eye, bright blue.

Panzer-man, panzer-man, O You——

Not God but a swastika

So black no sky could squeak through.

Every woman adores a Fascist,

The boot in the face, the brute

Brute heart of a brute like you.

You stand at the blackboard, daddy,

In the picture I have of you,

A cleft in your chin instead of your foot

But no less a devil for that, no not

Any less the black man who

Bit my pretty red heart in two.

I was ten when they buried you.

At twenty I tried to die

And get back, back, back to you.

I thought even the bones would do.

But they pulled me out of the sack,

And they stuck me together with glue.

And then I knew what to do.

I made a model of you,

A man in black with a Meinkampf look

And a love of the rack and the screw.

And I said I do, I do.

So daddy, I'm finally through.

The black telephone's off at the root,

The voices just can't worm through.

If I've killed one man, I've killed two——

The vampire who said he was you

And drank my blood for a year,

Seven years, if you want to know.

Daddy, you can lie back now.

There's a stake in your fat black heart

And the villagers never liked you.

They are dancing and stamping on you.

They always *knew* it was you.

Daddy, daddy, you bastard, I'm through.

From *Ariel*

*T*he death of Otto Plath intensified young Sylvia's sense of insecurity. Because the Plaths were left with very little money, they moved in with Aurelia Plath's parents in Wellesley, Massachusetts. Aurelia returned to teaching full time, and the children were left in the care of their grandparents. Sylvia had lost her father, and in a sense she had lost her mother too. For the rest of her life Sylvia would struggle with feelings of resentment toward Aurelia, partly because she despised the dependency her mother brought out in her.

More determined than ever to get attention, Sylvia threw herself into her schoolwork and extracurricular activities. In junior and senior high school she earned nearly perfect grades and amassed academic awards and honors, all while editing the school newspaper and participating in sports and the orchestra. At the end of high school she won scholarships to attend prestigious Smith College in Northampton, Massachusetts; there she added to her "golden girl" image by dating a handsome pre-med student at Yale. Sylvia seemed remarkably well-adjusted to everyone who knew her, but she was never satisfied with her accomplishments. In her diary she wrote, "Never never never will I reach the perfection I long for with all my soul."

Excellent grades, awards, popularity—Sylvia pursued them all ardently. But there was one thing that was more important to her than all of these: her writing. She was only eight when her first poem was published in the *Boston Sunday Herald*. By the time she started college, she had sold pieces to *Seventeen* and *The Christian Science Monitor*. She was passionate about writing and would not rest until she was a famous writer.

A page from Plath's high school diary.

THE DISQUIETING MUSES

*M*other, mother, what illbred aunt

Or what disfigured and unsightly

Cousin did you so unwisely keep

Unasked to my christening, that she

Sent these ladies in her stead

With heads like darning-eggs to nod

And nod and nod at foot and head

And at the left side of my crib?

Mother, who made to order stories

Of Mixie Blackshort the heroic bear,

Mother, whose witches always, always

Got baked into gingerbread, I wonder

Whether you saw them, whether you said

Words to rid me of those three ladies

Nodding by night around my bed,

Mouthless, eyeless, with stitched bald head.

(continued)

In the hurricane, when father's twelve
Study windows bellied in
Like bubbles about to break, you fed
My brother and me cookies and Ovaltine
And helped the two of us to choir:
"Thor is angry: boom boom boom!
Thor is angry: we don't care!"
But those ladies broke the panes.

When on tiptoe the schoolgirls danced,
Blinking flashlights like fireflies
And singing the glowworm song, I could
Not lift a foot in the twinkle-dress
But, heavy-footed, stood aside
In the shadow cast by my dismal-headed
Godmothers, and you cried and cried:
And the shadow stretched, the lights went out.

Mother, you sent me to piano lessons
And praised my arabesques and trills
Although each teacher found my touch
Oddly wooden in spite of scales
And the hours of practicing, my ear
Tone-deaf and yes, unteachable.
I learned, I learned, I learned elsewhere,
From muses unhired by you, dear mother,

I woke one day to see you, mother,
Floating above me in bluest air
On a green balloon bright with a million
Flowers and bluebirds that never were
Never, never, found anywhere.
But the little planet bobbed away
Like a soap-bubble as you called: Come here!
And I faced my traveling companions.

(continued)

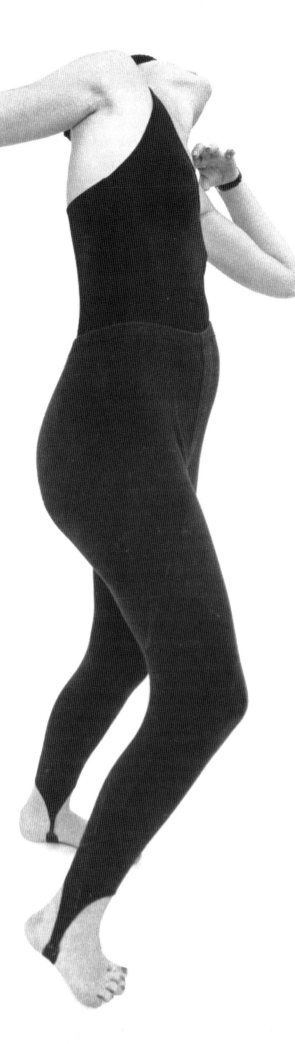

Day now, night now, at head, side, feet,

They stand their vigil in gowns of stone,

Faces blank as the day I was born,

Their shadows long in the setting sun

That never brightens or goes down.

And this is the kingdom you bore me to,

Mother, mother. But no frown of mine

Will betray the company I keep.

From *The Colossus*

During her first two years at Smith College, Sylvia continued to succeed at nearly everything she tried. But her junior year was plagued with difficulties. For financial reasons, she was forced to move out of her familiar dormitory and into a "scholarship house," where she had to prepare food, wait tables, and work as a receptionist in exchange for room and board. Many of her closest friends had left school, her relationship with her boyfriend was uncertain, and even her classes were disappointing. As the months passed, she became more and more depressed. One of her journal entries from November 1952 shows her frustration:

> I fell into bed again this morning, begging for sleep, withdrawing into the dark, warm, fetid escape from action, from responsibility…I thought of the myriad of physical duties I have to perform…The list mounted obstacle after fiendish obstacle; they jarred, they leered, they fell apart in chaos, and the revulsion, the desire to end the pointless round of objects, of things, of actions, rose higher…

Despite her terrible anxiety and self-doubt, Sylvia continued to publish her poems and short stories and to win awards. In the spring she learned that she was one of only twenty college women in the country chosen to guest edit the August 1953 issue of *Mademoiselle* magazine. The experience of living and working in New York City proved to be more exhausting than glamorous, however, and Sylvia's confidence was shaken still further by the tough, demanding editor of the magazine.

Upon her return from New York, her fragile ego received another blow: She had not been accepted to a summer fiction course at Harvard that she had counted on attending. Feeling like a complete failure, Sylvia dreaded the empty summer at home with her mother.

College Hall at Smith College.

This is the light of the mind, cold and planetary.

The trees of the mind are black. The light is blue.

The grasses unload their griefs on my feet

    as if I were God,

Prickling my ankles and murmuring of their humility.

Fumy, spiritous mists inhabit this place

Separated from my house by a row of headstones.

I simply cannot see where there is to get to.

The moon is no door. It is a face in its own right,

White as a knuckle and terribly upset.

It drags the sea after it like a dark crime; it is quiet

With the O-gape of complete despair. I live here.

Twice on Sunday, the bells startle the sky——

Eight great tongues affirming the Resurrection.

At the end, they soberly bong out their names.

The yew tree points up. It has a Gothic shape.

The eyes lift after it and find the moon.

The moon is my mother. She is not sweet like Mary.

Her blue garments unloose small bats and owls.

How I would like to believe in tenderness——

The face of the effigy, gentled by candles,

Bending, on me in particular, its mild eyes.

I have fallen a long way. Clouds are flowering

Blue and mystical over the face of the stars.

Inside the church, the saints will be all blue,

Floating on their delicate feet over the cold pews,

Their hands and faces stiff with holiness.

The moon sees nothing of this. She is bald and wild.

And the message of the yew tree is blackness—

    blackness and silence.

From *Ariel*

A SUICIDE ATTEMPT

*A*urelia Plath knew that her daughter was unhappy during the summer of 1953, but she was thoroughly unprepared for the shock she received when Sylvia wandered into the kitchen one morning with self-inflicted gashes on her legs. "I just wanted to see if I had the guts!" Sylvia said. Then she seized Aurelia's hands and cried, "Oh, Mother, the world is too rotten! I want to die! Let's die together!"

Aurelia immediately took her daughter to a psychiatrist, who recommended electroshock therapy. Sylvia received no preparation before the treatments and no counseling afterwards, and she found the experience frightening and painful. Furthermore, the therapy did not cure her terrible depression.

On August 24, Sylvia crept into a crawl space in the basement of her Wellesley home and consumed most of a bottle of sleeping pills. When Aurelia could not find Sylvia, an intensive search was launched. The disappearance of the "Beautiful Smith Girl" even received national news coverage.

Almost two days later Sylvia's brother Warren heard the distant sound of moaning under the house. He rushed downstairs, peered into the crawl space, and found his sister, half-conscious but physically unharmed. An ambulance took Sylvia to the hospital, where she began several months of psychiatric treatment.

Sylvia later wrote about her suicide attempt in *The Bell Jar*. By the end of the novel the heroine, Esther, has been "patched, retreaded, and approved for the road." Like Esther, Sylvia seemed well when she finally emerged from the hospital in February 1954. But it was really only a reprieve.

A dim, undersea light filtered through the slits of the cellar windows. Behind the oil burner, a dark gap showed in the wall at about shoulder height and ran back under the breezeway, out of sight. The breezeway had been added to the house after the cellar was dug, and built out over this secret, earth-bottomed crevice.

A few old, rotting fireplace logs blocked the hole mouth. I shoved them back a bit. Then I set the glass of water and the bottle of pills side by side on the flat surface of one of the logs and started to heave myself up.

It took me a good while to heft my body into the gap, but at last, after many tries, I managed it, and crouched at the mouth of the darkness, like a troll.

The earth seemed friendly under my bare feet, but cold. I wondered how long it had been since this particular square of soil had seen the sun.

Then, one after the other, I lugged the heavy, dust-covered logs across the hole mouth. The dark felt thick as velvet. I reached for the glass and bottle, and carefully, on my knees, with bent head, crawled to the farthest wall.

Cobwebs touched my face with the softness of moths. Wrapping my black coat round me like my own sweet shadow, I unscrewed the bottle of pills and started taking them swiftly, between gulps of water, one by one by one.

At first nothing happened, but as I approached the bottom of the bottle, red and blue lights began to flash before my eyes. The bottle slid from my fingers and I lay down.

The silence drew off, baring the pebbles and shells and all the tatty wreckage of my life. Then, at the rim of vision, it gathered itself, and in one sweeping tide, rushed me to sleep.

From *The Bell Jar*

STARTING OVER

When Sylvia returned to Smith College after her months of hospitalization, she was idolized by many of the younger students as a romantic figure—a brilliant, sophisticated woman who had suffered a nervous breakdown. Sylvia began writing again, turning out dozens of poems and several short stories, and her success in publishing them in such magazines as *Harper's* and *The Atlantic Monthly* added to her glamour.

With her statuesque figure, dark eyes, and hair newly lightened to a striking blonde, Sylvia was also very attractive to men, and she became involved in a series of affairs. Partly because many of her friends were getting married, she felt an almost panicky need to find a mate for herself. Sylvia was willing to conform to society's expectations for a woman in the 1950s, but only up to a point: She would find a husband as soon as possible, but, as a married woman, she would not abandon her own goals and ambitions.

Sylvia's career at Smith ended with an incredible array of honors and prizes. Her most important award was a Fulbright fellowship to Newnham College at Cambridge University in England. In September 1955 Sylvia, now almost twenty-three, sailed for Europe with enthusiasm and optimism. It was good to put so much distance between herself and her recent past.

September 1955: Plath with her brother, Warren, shortly before she departed for Cambridge.

THE APPLICANT

*F*irst, are you our sort of a person?

Do you wear

A glass eye, false teeth or a crutch,

A brace or a hook,

Rubber breasts or a rubber crotch,

Stitches to show something's missing? No, no? Then

How can we give you a thing?

Stop crying.

Open your hand.

Empty? Empty. Here is a hand

To fill it and willing

To bring teacups and roll away headaches

And do whatever you tell it.

Will you marry it?

It is guaranteed

To thumb shut your eyes at the end

And dissolve of sorrow.

We make new stock from the salt.

I notice you are stark naked.

How about this suit——

(continued)

Black and stiff, but not a bad fit.

Will you marry it?

It is waterproof, shatterproof, proof

Against fire and bombs through the roof.

Believe me, they'll bury you in it.

Now your head, excuse me, is empty.

I have the ticket for that.

Come here, sweetie, out of the closet.

Well, what do you think of *that*?

Naked as paper to start

But in twenty-five years she'll be silver,

In fifty, gold.

A living doll, everywhere you look.

It can sew, it can cook,

It can talk, talk, talk.

It works, there is nothing wrong with it.

You have a hole, it's a poultice.

You have an eye, it's an image.

My boy, it's your last resort.

Will you marry it, marry it, marry it.

From *Ariel*

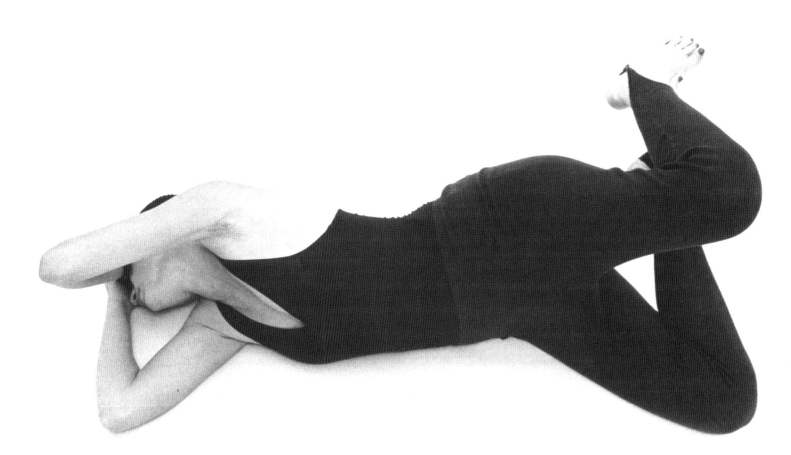

MARRIAGE

*P*lath was to spend most of the rest of her life in England. Although she never became accustomed to the chilly, damp weather, in most respects, Cambridge was a delightful change for her. The literary atmosphere was inspiring, and Plath's social life was very full. Many men were attracted to the intense American poet, but she was never completely satisfied with any of them. Then, in February 1956, she read some poems by an Englishman named Ted Hughes. She met Hughes that same night at a party. Plath realized almost immediately that he was her ideal, both physically and intellectually. She described him in a letter to her mother as "the strongest man in the world, ex-Cambridge, brilliant poet whose work I loved before I met him, a large, hulking, healthy Adam . . . with a voice like the thunder of God."

Passionately in love, Plath and Hughes married on June 16, 1956, in London. Her mother was the only guest; Plath had decided to keep the wedding secret because she thought it was against the rules of her Fulbright fellowship. In fact, after a honeymoon in Spain, they actually lived apart for several weeks to conceal their union. But separation was too much for the newlyweds to bear, and Plath finally told the college authorities, who were sympathetic after all.

Although Plath was happy with her marriage, she was frequently exhausted by her new responsibilities. Besides doing the cooking and cleaning, she chose to act as Ted's business manager, typing and sending out his poems. She sometimes resented the time these tasks took away from her own studying and writing; she also was frustrated, as always, by her inability to do everything perfectly. Her stress was aggravated by worries about money. It was a relief, then, when she completed her final examinations at Cambridge and received an offer from Smith College to return to the United States and teach.

LOVE LETTER

*N*ot easy to state the change you made.

If I'm alive now, then I was dead,

Though, like a stone, unbothered by it,

Staying put according to habit.

You didn't just toe me an inch, no—

Nor leave me to set my small bald eye

Skyward again, without hope, of course,

Of apprehending blueness, or stars.

That wasn't it. I slept, say: a snake

Masked among black rocks as a black rock

In the white hiatus of winter—

Like my neighbors, taking no pleasure

In the million perfectly-chiseled

Cheeks alighting each moment to melt

My cheek of basalt. They turned to tears,

Angels weeping over dull natures,

But didn't convince me. Those tears froze.

Each dead head had a visor of ice.

And I slept on like a bent finger.

The first thing I saw was sheer air

And the locked drops rising in a dew

Limpid as spirits. Many stones lay

Dense and expressionless around about.

I didn't know what to make of it.

I shone, mica-scaled, and unfolded

To pour myself out like a fluid

Among bird feet and the stems of plants.

I wasn't fooled. I knew you at once.

Tree and stone glittered, without shadows.

My finger-length grew lucent as glass.

I started to bud like a March twig:

An arm and a leg, an arm, a leg.

From stone to cloud, so I ascended.

Now I resemble a sort of god

Floating through the air in my soul-shift

Pure as a pane of ice. It's a gift.

From *Crossing the Water*

*T*eaching was one more thing that Plath believed she failed at, although in reality she did it very well. Her students thought she was dramatic and impressive, but she felt ill at ease in the classroom. The job also demanded far more of her time than she had expected. As the months passed, Plath became more and more certain that she could be happy only if she could write full time.

After a year, Plath resigned her teaching position and settled into a Boston apartment with her husband. She was ready to devote herself to her writing, but once again, she met with disappointment. Now that she finally had the time to write, she simply couldn't do it. Her writer's block lasted for several months, fueled by the old fears of inadequacy and by anxiety over money.

Deciding that she needed help, Plath went to see the therapist who had supervised her recovery six years before. With the doctor's guidance, she at long last began to work through the grief and rage caused by her father's death. She also began to understand her resentment of her mother, which grew out of early feelings of rivalry and was aggravated by an unshakable emotional dependence. After a year of therapy, she began to feel more comfortable with herself and began to write again.

During the autumn of 1959, Plath and Hughes spent two months at a writer's colony in Saratoga Springs, New York. Relieved of housework and financial worries, Plath finally had the time and energy to find her true poetic voice—bold, slangy, distinctly American. As she noted in her journal, she was being "true to her own weirdnesses." The poems she wrote that fall would be collected in her first work, *The Colossus and Other Poems.*

The poets at Cape Cod, 1958.

I shall never get you put together entirely,

Pieced, glued, and properly jointed.

Mule-bray, pig-grunt and bawdy cackles

Proceed from your great lips.

It's worse than a barnyard.

Perhaps you consider yourself an oracle,

Mouthpiece of the dead, or of some god or other.

Thirty years now I have labored

To dredge the silt from your throat.

I am none the wiser.

Scaling little ladders with gluepots and pails of lysol

I crawl like an ant in mourning

Over the weedy acres of your brow

To mend the immense skull plates and clear

The bald, white tumuli of your eyes.

(continued)

A blue sky out of the Oresteia

Arches above us. O father, all by yourself

You are pithy and historical as the Roman Forum.

I open my lunch on a hill of black cypress.

Your fluted bones and acanthine hair are littered

In their old anarchy to the horizon-line.

It would take more than a lightning-stroke

To create such a ruin.

Nights, I squat in the cornucopia

Of your left ear, out of the wind,

Counting the red stars and those of plum-color.

The sun rises under the pillar of your tongue.

My hours are married to shadow.

No longer do I listen for the scrape of a keel

On the blank stones of the landing.

From the collection *The Colossus*

*B*ack in London in the spring of 1960, Plath turned her considerable energies to motherhood. On April 1 she gave birth to a daughter, Frieda. After a very upsetting miscarriage the following year, she had a son, Nicholas, in 1962.

Plath was a loving, proud mother. Most of the poems she wrote about her children are gentler and more joyful than her other works. Ted Hughes believed that, with Frieda's birth, his wife finally arrived "at her own center of gravity." But motherhood was also a burden for Plath; although Hughes helped, the responsibility for the children was largely hers. Added to her other domestic duties, the care of her children left Plath very little time to write poems or work on her novel, *The Bell Jar.* Hughes's fame was growing—he was publishing regularly and recording programs for the BBC—but Plath was known to many people, even in London literary circles, as simply "Mrs. Hughes."

By the time Frieda was a year old, it had become obvious that the growing family needed more space. The tiny London flat had become oppressive to the couple, and the distractions of city living interfered with their writing. To their delight they found an ancient ten-room house, with a thatched roof and a backyard orchard, for sale in the tiny village of Devon, England. They moved in at the end of August 1961.

Plath had looked forward to the move with great optimism, but she again suffered disappointment. Although the house was charming, it was run-down and lacked modern conveniences. Caring for it left her perpetually exhausted. On good days she could be inspired by her new surroundings; as time passed, however, they began to seem more and more bleak.

*C*lownlike, happiest on your hands,

Feet to the stars, and moon-skulled,

Gilled like a fish. A common-sense

Thumbs-down on the dodo's mode.

Wrapped up in yourself like a spool,

Trawling your dark as owls do.

Mute as a turnip from the Fourth

Of July to All Fools' Day,

O high-riser, my little loaf.

Vague as fog and looked for like mail.

Farther off than Australia.

Bent-backed Atlas, our travelled prawn.

Snug as a bud and at home

Like a sprat in a pickle jug.

A creel of eels, all ripples.

Jumpy as a Mexican bean.

Right, like a well-done sum.

A clean slate, with your own face on.

From *Ariel*

*T*hroughout their marriage, Plath and Hughes were together nearly all the time, working under the same roof. Plath guarded their close relationship jealously, sometimes succumbing to fits of rage when other people intruded upon it. Usually the threats that she perceived were not real, but in the summer of 1962 she discovered that her husband was attracted to, and possibly already having an affair with, the wife of another poet.

Overwhelmed with grief and anger, Plath built a bonfire in front of their home and fed it with Hughes's letters and drafts of his poems. She also tore the telephone wires from the wall after intercepting a call from her rival. Over the next few months Plath agonized about whether her marriage could, or should, be saved. Her moods swung wildly, from hysteria one day to an amazingly calm acceptance the next. Finally she either asked Hughes to go, or he made the decision to leave himself. In early October he moved out.

Plath turned to writing as an outlet for her pain. The resulting poems, churned out at a furious pace, were the finest she had ever written. They would be published after her death as the collection *Ariel*.

In one of the *Ariel* poems, "Stings," Plath wrote, "I have a self to recover, a queen." Although she mourned the end of her marriage, she was gaining a new sense of freedom and power through her writing. It seemed to her that it was time to leave the isolation of Devon and get out into the world again. In December 1962 she and the children returned to London.

Devon, 1962: Plath and her mother pose with Frieda and Nicholas.

Bare-handed, I hand the combs.

The man in white smiles, bare-handed,

Our cheesecloth gauntlets neat and sweet,

The throats of our wrists brave lilies.

He and I

Have a thousand clean cells between us,

Eight combs of yellow cups,

And the hive itself a teacup,

White with pink flowers on it,

With excessive love I enameled it

Thinking 'Sweetness, sweetness'.

Brood cells gray as the fossils of shells

Terrify me, they seem so old.

What am I buying, wormy mahogany?

Is there any queen at all in it?

If there is, she is old,

Her wings torn shawls, her long body

Rubbed of its plush——

Poor and bare and unqueenly and even shameful.

I stand in a column

Of winged, unmiraculous women,

Honey-drudgers.

I am no drudge

Though for years I have eaten dust

And dried plates with my dense hair.

And seen my strangeness evaporate,

Blue dew from dangerous skin.

Will they hate me,

These women who only scurry,

Whose news is the open cherry, the open clover?

It is almost over.

I am in control.

Here is my honey-machine,

It will work without thinking,

Opening, in spring, like an industrious virgin

To scour the creaming crests

As the moon, for its ivory powders, scours the sea.

A third person is watching.

He has nothing to do with the bee-seller or with me.

Now he is gone

(continued)

In eight great bounds, a great scapegoat.

Here is his slipper, here is another,

And here the square of white linen

He wore instead of a hat.

He was sweet,

The sweat of his efforts a rain

Tugging the world to fruit.

The bees found him out,

Molding onto his lips like lies,

Complicating his features.

They thought death was worth it, but I

Have a self to recover, a queen.

Is she dead, is she sleeping?

Where has she been,

With her lion-red body, her wings of glass?

Now she is flying

More terrible than she ever was, red

Scar in the sky, red comet

Over the engine that killed her——

The mausoleum, the wax house.

From *Ariel*

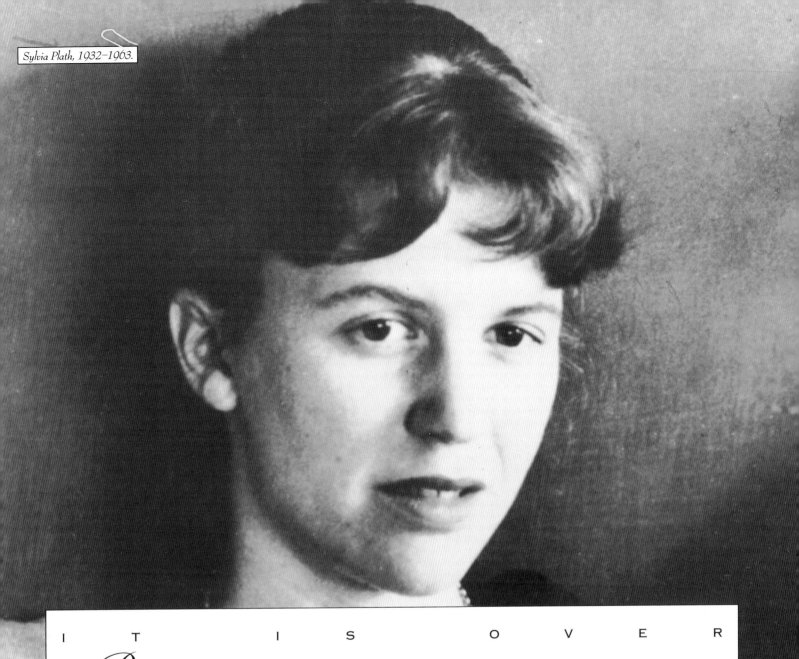

Sylvia Plath, 1932–1963.

IT IS OVER

*P*lath was hopeful about the future when she moved into her new London flat at the end of 1962, but her optimism was short-lived. The winter was one of the harshest London had ever known. Trapped inside by the weather and unable to get telephone service, she felt almost as isolated as she had in Devon. Even the British publication of *The Bell Jar* in January offered little consolation. Although she began to see a doctor, she sank into a terrible, all-too-familiar depression.

Early on the morning of February 11, 1963, Plath left cups of milk beside Nicholas and Frieda's beds. Next she put tape around the doors and stuffed towels under them to protect the sleeping children. Then she went into the kitchen, knelt by the oven, turned on the gas, and put her head inside. Later that morning a nurse, sent by Plath's doctor, found her dead.

Only thirty years old, Plath may have decided at least a week earlier that she was ready to die. On February 5, in what was probably her last poem, "Edge," she noted, "We have come so far, it is over." But with her death, Plath's legend was just beginning.

By revealing so much of herself in her poetry, Sylvia Plath offered up not only her work, but also her life, for close scrutiny. Her story still fascinates people because it is about love and death, success and failure, joy and sorrow—a life lived intensely.

The woman is perfected.

Her dead

Body wears the smile of accomplishment,

The illusion of a Greek necessity

Flows in the scrolls of her toga,

Her bare

Feet seem to be saying:

We have come so far, it is over.

Each dead child coiled, a white serpent,

One at each little

Pitcher of milk, now empty.

She has folded

Them back into her body as petals

Of a rose close when the garden

Stiffens and odors bleed

From the sweet, deep throats of the night flower.

The moon has nothing to be sad about,

Staring from her hood of bone.

She is used to this sort of thing.

Her blacks crackle and drag.

From *Ariel*

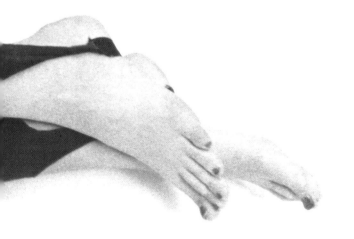

ACKNOWLEDGMENTS

Edited by S. L. Berry and Nancy Loewen
Photo research by Ann Schwab
Design assistant: Mindy Belter

PHOTO CREDITS

POETRY CREDITS

SELECTED WORKS BY SYLVIA PLATH

POETRY
The Colossus, 1960
Ariel, 1965
Crossing the Water, 1971
Crystal Gazer & Other Poems, 1971
Winter Trees, 1972
Collected Poems, 1981

PROSE
The Bell Jar, 1963
*Johnny Panic and the Bible of Dreams: Short
  Stories, Prose and Diary Excerpts,* 1979

INDEX

Published by Creative Education

123 South Broad Street, Mankato, Minnesota 56001

Creative Education is an imprint of Creative Education, Inc.

Copyright © 1994 Creative Education, Inc.

International copyrights reserved in all countries.

No part of this book may be reproduced in any form without

written permission from the publisher.

Printed in Italy.

Art Direction: Rita Marshall

Designed by: Stephanie Blumenthal

Photographs © 1993 Benno Friedman

Library of Congress Cataloging-in-Publication Data

Chapman, Lynne F. (Lynne Ferguson)

    Sylvia Plath / written by Lynne F. Chapman.

       p. cm. -- (Voices in poetry)

    Includes bibliographical references (p.) and index.

    Summary: A biography of the troubled woman whose literary

achievements were cut short by her suicide at age thirty, inter-

spersed with examples of her poetry.

    ISBN 0-88682-614-4

    1. Plath, Sylvia--Biography--Juvenile literature.   2. Poets,

American--20th century--Biography--Juvenile literature.   3.

Young adult poetry, American.   [1. Plath, Sylvia.

2. Poets, American.   3. American poetry.]   I. Title.   II. Series:

Voices in poetry (Mankato, Minn.)

PS3566.L27Z6   1993   93-3354

811'.54--dc20   CIP

[B]   AC